C000226835

Introduction

The Union Flag is one of the best-known national symbols in the world. This is not surprising as it has been around for over 400 years with only minor changes. The Union Flag signifies the unity of the nations that make up the United Kingdom and dependencies, and demonstrates the bonds of citizenship which we all share. Whatever our differences may be, whatever our faith, culture, political views, ethnicity, first language or traditional customs, we can all stand beneath this flag united together in common purpose.

But for too long our flag has been taken for granted and largely ignored. Few children are taught about it in school, few people know its history or even the correct way to fly it. It is time that this changed and we became familiar with our flag, because all of us have the right to fly the flag and may use it on land wherever and whenever we wish. It is the people's flag as well as the state flag.

The Flag Institute, in association with the Flags & Heraldry Committee, an all party group of the United Kingdom Parliament, has produced this booklet to help and guide you when flying the flag in a variety of situations - it provides a few simple rules to ensure that the flag is flown correctly and is treated with dignity and respect.

We would like to pay tribute to Graham Bartram, Chief Vexillologist of the Flag Institute, for his outstanding graphics and detailed knowledge in the drafting of this booklet, and also to officials at the Department for Culture, Media and Sport (DCMS) who so kindly supported this venture.

Above all we hope this booklet will encourage you to fly your flag with affection and pride.

Malcolm Farrow OBE
President of the Flag Institute

Andrew Rosindell MP
Chairman of the Flags & Heraldry Committee

March 2010

1

Flying Flags in the United Kingdom - A Guide to Britain's Flag Protocol

First published in the United Kingdom in 2010 by the Flag Institute in association with the Flags and Heraldry Committee of the UK Parliament and with support from the Department for Culture, Media and Sport.

Copyright © The Flag Institute 2010

Graham Bartram has asserted his rights under the Copyright, Designs and Patent Act 1988 and the Berne Convention on Copyright to be identified as the author of this work.

All rights reserved. No part of this booklet may be reproduced, stored in a retrieval system or transmitted in any way or by any means, electronic, mechanical, photocopying, recording or otherwise without the prior written permission of the copyright holder.

Whilst every care has been taken in the preparation of this booklet, neither the publishers nor the author assume any responsibility for errors or omissions, or for damages resulting from the use of the information contained herein.

ISBN 978-0-9513286-1-3

Printed and bound in the United Kingdom by printing.com.

Image Credits

Illustrations: Graham Bartram

Front Cover: Donald Edwards

Inside Front Cover (left to right, top to bottom): Adrian Dennis - AFP; Malcolm Farrow; René Mansi[†]; Douglas Freer[†]; Dan Kite[†]; Arthur M; Matthew Dixon[†]; Marek Slusarczyk[†]; Donald Edwards

Page 1: Paul Kemp

Inside Back Cover (left to right, top to bottom): Graham Heywood[†]; Colin Dobson; Arthur M; Mark Bridge; Jim Oatway; Don Bayley[†]; Graham Bartram; ditto; ditto

[†] from iStockPhoto.com

The Union Flag

The national flag of the United Kingdom, the Crown Dependencies and Overseas Territories is the Union Flag, which may also be called the Union Jack.[1] The first Union Flag was created in 1606 and combined the flags of England and Scotland. The present Union Flag dates from 1801 when St. Patrick's Cross was added to represent Ireland. It then became possible to display the flag upside down. There is no Flag Act in UK law and the Union Flag is the national flag by long established custom and practice, rather than by statute.

The First Union Flag

The Flag Protocol of the United Kingdom

The national flags of the United Kingdom (ie. the Union Flag and the flags of England, Scotland and Wales) should be displayed only in a dignified manner befitting the national emblems. They should not be displayed in a position inferior to any other flag or ensign.

It is improper to use the national flags as a table or seat cover or as a masking for boxes, barriers, or the intervening space between a dais or platform and the floor. The use of any of the national flags to cover a statue, monument or plaque for an unveiling ceremony is discouraged.

Flying the Flag

Flags may be flown on every day of the year. Government and local authority buildings in England, Scotland and Wales are encouraged to fly national flags every day of the year (the flying of flags at certain locations in Northern Ireland is constrained by *The Flags Regulations [Northern Ireland] 2000* and *Police Emblems and Flag Regulations [Northern Ireland] 2002*).[2]

The Modern Union Flag

Flags are normally flown from sunrise to sunset but they may also be flown at night, when they should be illuminated.

No permission is needed to fly the national flags and they are excluded from most planning and advertising regulations (but flagpoles may not be).

National flags should never be flown in a worn or damaged condition, or when soiled. To do so is to show disrespect for the nations they represent.

Important: the Union Flag has a correct way up - in the half of the flag nearest the flagpole, the wider diagonal white stripe must be above the red diagonal stripe, as Scotland's St Andrew's Cross takes precedence over Ireland's St. Patrick's Cross. It is most improper to fly the flag upside down.

If a purely decorative effect is desired it is better to confine the display to flags of lesser status; for example, house flags, pennants or coloured bunting.

This flag is upside down!

Position of Honour

The order of precedence of flags in the UK is: Royal Standards, the Union Flag, the flag of the host country (England, Scotland, Wales, etc.), flags of other nations (in alphabetical order, see the list on page 15), the Commonwealth Flag, the European Union Flag, county flags, flags of cities or towns, banners of arms, and house flags. See Appendix B (page 13) for a detailed precedence list and special precedence orders for international organizations.

When British national flags are flown with the flags of other nations each flag should be the same size (or have the same width - the measure-

---

1 See Hansard - House of Lords Debate 14 July 1908 vol 192 cc 579 - 80.
2 See www.opsi.gov.uk/Sr/sr2000/nisr_20000347_en.pdf & www.opsi.gov.uk/Sr/sr2002/20020023.htm

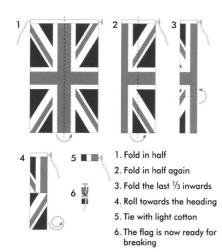

1. Fold in half
2. Fold in half again
3. Fold the last ⅓ inwards
4. Roll towards the heading
5. Tie with light cotton
6. The flag is now ready for breaking

Folding a Flag for Breaking

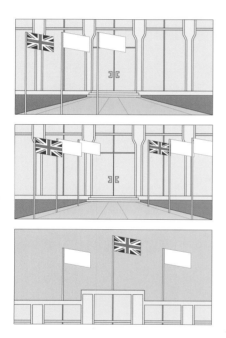

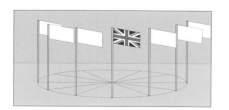

ment from top to bottom) and should fly from a separate flagpole of the same height.[3] The UK's flag shape of 3:5 works well with nearly all other nations' flags and it is recommended to use these proportions if a standard size is required for all the flags in a display.[4]

The senior British national flag (eg. the Union Flag or the flag of England, Scotland or Wales) should be raised first and lowered last, unless all the flags can be raised and lowered simultaneously. Flags should be raised and lowered in a dignified manner. An alternative British tradition for flag raising is to hoist the flag while rolled up and secured with a thin piece of cotton or a slip knot. A sharp tug of the halyard will break the cotton and release the flag to fly free. This is known as 'breaking' the flag, and is sometimes used to signal the beginning of an event, or the arrival of a VIP.

National flags should be displayed as follows:

In Front of and On a Building

Where there are two or more flagpoles parallel to the building line, the senior national flag should be the first flag on the left of an observer facing the main entrance of the building. The remaining flags then appear in order of precedence from left to right.

Where there are two or more flagpoles on the forecourt of a building angled to the main entrance, the senior national flag should be flown on the outermost pole when the flagpoles are to the left of the main entrance and on the innermost pole when the flagpoles are to the right of the main entrance, as shown in the diagram.

If only one flag is to be flown and there are two flagpoles, it should be flown on the flagpole to the observer's left. If there are more than two flagpoles, it should be flown as near as possible to the centre. This only applies when the other flagpoles remain empty. It is permissible to fly the same national flag on more than one flagpole by repeating the order of precedence.

If one flagpole is higher than the rest, then the senior national flag can fly from that flagpole; however no non-UK national flags can be flown on the other flagpoles. These can be used for more junior flags such as county and house flags. Alternatively the higher flagpole can be left empty and the remaining flagpoles used. In general when siting flagpoles it is preferable to keep them at the same level to avoid protocol restrictions.

The appropriate size of flag for any flagpole is a matter of aesthetics but, as a guide, a ground-level flagpole should have a flag whose length (its longer dimension) is no more than ⅓ of the pole's height. A flagpole on top of a building may need a larger flag because of the added height of the building.

Within a Circle of Flags

In a semi-circle of flags representing a number of nations, the senior national flag should be in the centre. The remaining flags should be placed with the next most senior flag (or first in alphabetical order if all the flags are of equal seniority) on the left of the central flag, the next on the right of the central flag, the next on the 2nd left from the central flag, and continuing to alternate left and right.

---

3   International protocol prohibits the flying of any nation's flag higher than another (apart from at medal ceremonies during sporting events).
4   If each country's official dimensions are being used, any of the flags that are square or nearly square can have a slightly larger width (up to 25% more) to give a more equal area.

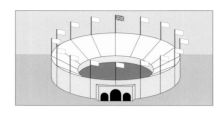

In an enclosed circle of flags representing a number of nations, the senior national flag should be flown on the flagpole immediately opposite the main entrance to the venue, or above the Royal Box if there is no main entrance. The remaining flags should be arranged as for the semi-circle of flags described above. Alternatively they can be arranged alphabetically, going clockwise.

From a Flagpole with Yardarm and Gaff

When displayed on a flagpole fitted with yardarms (horizontal cross-pieces), the senior national flag or ensign[5] should be flown from the starboard yardarm (the right as viewed from the rear, the left as viewed from the front).

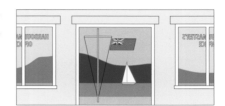

If the flagpole is fitted with a gaff (a short pole attached to the flagpole at an angle - see diagram), the senior *ensign* should be flown from the gaff. If there is no ensign to be flown, the gaff should be left empty and the senior national flag flown from the starboard yardarm, as described above.

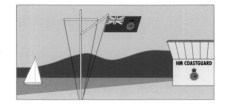

A yacht club burgee or distinguishing flag can be flown from the mast-head, the highest point of the flagpole.

In Processions

The senior national flag should always lead in a single file of flags.

When two or more flags are carried side-by-side, the senior national flag takes the position of honour at the right-hand side of the line facing the direction of movement (the left of an observer watching the line approach).

When passing the person taking the salute the flag should be lowered so that the staff is horizontal. This can be done by simply lowering the staff straight ahead, or by lowering the staff towards the person taking the salute and then swinging it round to straight ahead. All the movements should be slow and dignified. After the salute, the flag should be raised again.

With Crossed Flags

Whenever crossed with the flag of another nation or organization, the senior national flag should be on the left of the observer facing the flag. Its staff should be in front of the staff of the other flag.

Suspended Vertically Above a Street

Care should be taken to ensure that all flags suspended vertically across a street are hung to be seen from the same direction.

Flat Against a Surface

Union Flag - If hung horizontally or vertically, the broad white diagonal should be uppermost in the top-left corner.

Other flags - If hung vertically, the edge that would normally be the top of the flag should be on the left, so, for example, ensigns have their Union Flag canton in the upper left corner. On ensigns that have an armorial badge, if possible the badge should be upright, and the correct way round.

---

5 Ensigns are the national flags that identify a vessel's nationality and in the UK have the Union Flag in the top corner.

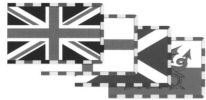

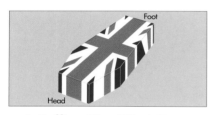

A Coffin with a Fitted Cover

(if a flag is used, 1:2 proportions fit the shape of the coffin better)

On a Speaker's Platform

When displayed from a staff, on a speaker's platform, the senior national flag should be placed on the right-hand side of the speaker, and therefore to the audience's left.

For interior or parade use a 'dress flag' may be used. This is sometimes made of silk or satin with a fringe around three sides. The fringe can be gold or red/white/blue for the Union Flag, red/white for St. George's Cross, blue/white for St. Andrew's Cross and green/white for the Red Dragon. The fringe is purely decorative.

Double-Flagging

Sometimes it may be desired to display two flags when only one flagpole is available. As long as both flags are British this is possible. The senior flag should fly at the top, with a gap of about 30cm (12"), assuming there is enough vertical space on the pole. For example, the Union Flag can be flown over the flag of England, Scotland or Wales (as shown), or over a county, city or house flag. When flags are at half-mast the lower flag must be removed.

As a Pall for a Coffin

If a national flag is to be used on a coffin, it should be placed so that the top-left corner of the flag is over the deceased's left shoulder. The flag should be removed before interment or cremation and folded.

If the flag is to be retained by the next of kin it can be folded using the Royal Navy's method shown here, based on a 1:2 flag (138cm x 276cm) with no fittings (ie. ropes, toggles or clips), or using the method shown on page 4:

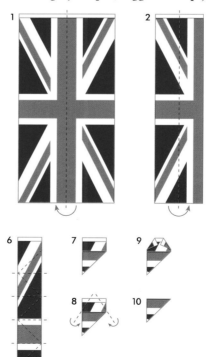

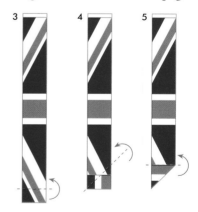

The Union Flag is pulled taut. The Union Flag is folded in half, lengthways (Fig. 1).

Keeping the Union Flag taught it is then folded in half (lengthways) a second time (Fig. 2).

A straight fold of 1/14 of the flag's length (20cm on a casket cover) is taken from the foot of the Union Flag (Fig. 3). This fold may not be necessary, or may need to be a different length, depending upon the shape, size and material of the flag being folded - practise first!

The first triangular fold is made ensuring it is within 5mm of the straight edge (Fig. 4).

The triangular folding procedure continues until it reaches the head of the Union Flag (Figs. 5, 6 & 7).

Any remainder is tucked away into the fold of the triangular shape (Fig. 8 & 9).

The Union Flag ready for presentation (Fig. 10).

On Vehicles

A car flag should be placed on a staff fitted to the front-right wing, in the centre of front edge of the bonnet, or in the centre of the front edge of the roof. If two flags are to be flown, the senior flag should be on the front-right wing and the junior flag on the front-left wing.

When flags are painted onto a vehicle, or on the tail fin of an aircraft, the flag on the port side should show the obverse of the flag (ie. the flagpole on the left), while that on the starboard side should show the reverse (ie. the flagpole on the right). On surfaces perpendicular to the direction of travel (eg. the back of the vehicle) the obverse of the flag should be shown.

On Uniforms

When flag shoulder patches are worn on uniforms the flag on the left shoulder or sleeve should show the obverse of the flag (ie. the flagpole at the wearer's front). If there is a patch on the right shoulder or sleeve it should show the reverse of the flag (ie. still with the flagpole at the wearer's front). If more than one flag is to be worn, the Union Flag should be at the top.

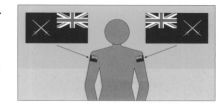

At Civilian Transport Facilities

Civilian marine facilities should fly the Civil Ensign (the undefaced Red Ensign) as their national flag, unless they belong to an organization that holds a warrant for a special ensign, when that ensign should be used instead.

Civilian air facilities, such as airports and airfields, should fly the Civil Air Ensign as their national flag, rather than the Union Flag. They may additionally fly the flag of England, Scotland or Wales and the appropriate county flag.

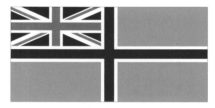

The Civil Air Ensign

Pennants

It is sometimes impractical to fly a full-size flag throughout the year - flags can wear out quickly, especially if they are flown in adverse conditions. Bare flagpoles are a sad sight. The pennant, or vimpel, is a solution to these problems. The long narrow streamer-like flags are designed to be left flying day and night. The optional single point attachment and the narrow tail reduce wear and their length means that they can be easily repaired.

Union

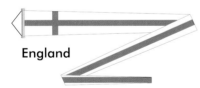

England

Scotland

Wales

The Royal Standard

The Royal Standard (actually the Royal Banner - a *standard* being an heraldic flag similar to the pennants above) should only be flown whilst the Royal person is on the premises, being hoisted (or broken) on their arrival and lowered following their departure. If the Royal person is to be present in a building, the Lord Chamberlain's Office or the Royal person's Private Secretary should be consulted. They will advise on the flag to be flown. The Royal Standard is never hoisted when the Royal person is passing in procession.

The Royal Standard
(in Scotland the design is different)

The Royal Standard takes precedence over all other flags in the United Kingdom, including the Union Flag.

A Stand of Flags at Full-mast

The Same Stand at Half-mast

Flags at Half-mast

Half-mast means the flag is flown two-thirds of the way up the flagpole, with at least the height of the flag between the top of the flag and the top of the flagpole. Flags cannot be flown at half-mast on poles that are more than 45° from the vertical, but a mourning cravat can be used instead (see below).

When a flag is to be flown at half-mast, it should first be raised all the way to the top of the mast, allowed to remain there for a second and then be lowered to the half-mast position. When it is being lowered from half-mast, it should again be raised to the top of the mast for a second before being fully lowered.

When a British national flag is at half-mast, other flags on the same stand of poles should also be at half-mast or should not be flown at all. Flags of foreign nations should not be flown, unless their country is also observing mourning.

The Royal Standard never flies at half-mast. It represents the Monarchy, which is continuous, and it would therefore be inappropriate for it to fly at half-mast.

Flags should be flown at half-mast on the following occasions:
a. From the announcement of the death until the funeral of the Sovereign, except on Proclamation Day when flags are flown at full-mast following the proclamation.
b. From the announcement of the death until the funeral of a member of the Royal Family styled 'Royal Highness', subject to special commands from the Sovereign in each case.
c. On the day of the announcement of the death and on the day of the funeral of other members of the Royal Family, subject to special commands from the Sovereign in each case.
d. The funerals of foreign Rulers, subject to special commands from the Sovereign in each case.
e. The funerals of Prime Ministers and ex-Prime Ministers of the United Kingdom, subject to special commands from the Sovereign in each case.
f. The funerals of First Ministers and ex-First Ministers of Scotland, Wales and Northern Ireland, subject to special commands from the Sovereign in each case. Unless otherwise commanded by the Sovereign, this only applies to flags in their respective countries.
g. At British Embassies, High Commissions and Missions when flags in the host country are flown at half-mast, subject to the discretion of the *Chef de Mission*.
h. Any other occasions where the Sovereign has given a special command.

If the body of a very distinguished citizen is lying in a building, the flag should fly at half-mast on that building until the body has left.

An alternative mark of mourning, used when half-masting is unsuitable, is to add a black cravat or ribbon to the top of the flag, at the hoist.

The above cover Royal and National Mourning, but flags may be flown at half-mast on private or non-Government buildings on other relevant occasions. Flags fly at full-mast on Remembrance Sunday.

Mourning Cravats

The Proper Disposal of Flags

When a flag becomes tattered or faded and is no longer in a suitable condition for use, it should be destroyed in a dignified way, for example by burning, tearing or cutting into strips that no longer resemble the original flag.

Appendix A - British Flags

A selection of the principal flags of the United Kingdom, British Overseas Territories and Crown Dependencies:

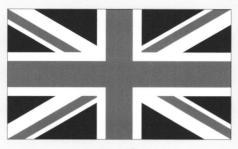

Union Flag

England

Scotland

Wales

Alderney

Anguilla

Bermuda

British Antarctic Territory

British Indian Ocean Territory

British Virgin Islands

Cayman Islands

Falkland Islands

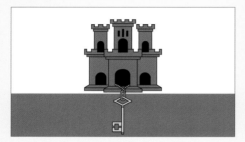

Gibraltar

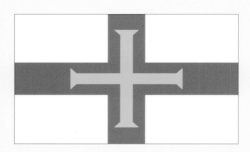

Guernsey

Isle of Man

Jersey

Montserrat

Pitcairn Islands

Saint Helena

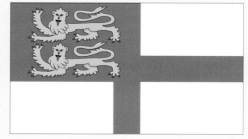

Sark

South Georgia and the South Sandwich Islands

Tristan da Cunha

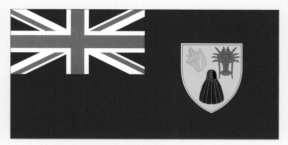

Turks and Caicos Islands

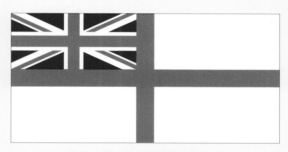

White Ensign (Royal Navy)

Royal Air Force Ensign

Red Ensign (Merchant Navy)

Civil Jack

Blue Ensign (Royal Fleet Auxiliary)

British Army (Non-Ceremonial)

Diplomatic Service Flag (eg. British Embassy)

Royal National Lifeboat Institution (RNLI)

HM Coastguard

United Kingdom Supreme Court

Trinity House (English and Welsh Lighthouses)

Northern Lights (Scottish Lighthouses)

Irish Lights (All Irish Lighthouses)

Metropolitan Police

Police Service of Northern Ireland (PSNI)

Ministry of Defence

Queen's Award for Enterprise

Appendix B - Precedence of Flags

There are four main orders of precedence for flags in the United Kingdom, depending upon the occasion:

General Precedence

The Royal Standards [6]
The Union Flag
The national flag of England, Scotland, Wales, a Crown Dependency or a British Overseas Territory (within those countries, dependencies or territories)
The White Ensign of the Royal Navy [7]
The Ensign of the Royal Air Force [7]
The Blue and Red Ensigns [7]
The Civil Air Ensign [7]
The national flags of England, Scotland, Wales, the Crown Dependencies and the British Overseas Territories (when displayed elsewhere)
The national flags of other nations (in English alphabetical order as shown on page 15)
The United Nations Flag
The Commonwealth Flag
The European Union Flag
The British Army Flag (Non-Ceremonial)
Flags of counties and metropolitan cities
Flags of other cities and towns
Banners of Arms (both personal and corporate)
House flags

Order for Commonwealth Events Held in the UK (but not the Commonwealth Games)

The Royal Standards [6]
The Commonwealth Flag
The Union Flag
The national flag of England, Scotland or Wales (whichever is hosting the event)
The national flags of the Commonwealth in order of original accession to the Commonwealth (date shown in brackets):

Canada (11 Dec 1931, dominion status 1867), Australia (11 Dec 1931, dominion status 1901), New Zealand (11 Dec 1931, dominion status 1907), South Africa (11 Dec 1931, dominion status 1910), India (14/15 Aug 1947), Pakistan (14/15 Aug 1947), Sri Lanka (4 Feb 1948), Ghana (6 Mar 1957), Malaysia (31 Aug 1957), Nigeria (1 Oct 1960), Cyprus (13 Mar 1961), Sierra Leone (27 Apr 1961), Tanzania (9 Dec 1961), Jamaica (6 Aug 1962), Trinidad and Tobago (31 Aug 1962), Uganda (9 Oct 1962), Kenya (12 Dec 1963), Malawi (6 Jul 1964), Malta (21 Sep 1964), Zambia (24 Oct 1964), The

The Commonwealth Flag

6 Only one Royal Standard is normally flown, and the order of precedence is: The Royal Standard of HM The Queen, The Personal Flags of HRH The Duke of Edinburgh, HRH The Prince of Wales and Duke of Rothesay, HRH Prince William of Wales, HRH Prince Harry of Wales, HRH The Duke of York, HRH The Earl of Wessex, HRH The Princess Royal, HRH The Duke of Gloucester, HRH The Duke of Kent, HRH Prince Michael of Kent, HRH Princess Alexandra, The Other Members' Standard.

7 When these ensigns are flown in place of the Union Flag they take the same precedence as the Union Flag.

Gambia (18 Feb 1965), Singapore (15 Oct 1965), Guyana (26 May 1966), Botswana (30 Sep 1966), Lesotho (4 Oct 1966), Barbados (30 Nov 1966), Mauritius (12 Mar 1968), Swaziland (6 Sep 1968), Nauru (1 Nov 1968), Tonga (4 Jun 1970), Samoa (28 Aug 1970), Fiji Islands (10 Oct 1970), Bangladesh (18 Apr 1972), The Bahamas (10 Jul 1973), Grenada (7 Feb 1974), Papua New Guinea (16 Sep 1975), Seychelles (29 Jun 1976), Solomon Islands (7 Jul 1978), Tuvalu (1 Oct 1978), Dominica (3 Nov 1978), Saint Lucia (22 Feb 1979), Kiribati (12 Jul 1979), Saint Vincent and the Grenadines (27 Oct 1979), Vanuatu (30 Jul 1980), Belize (21 Sep 1981), Antigua and Barbuda (1 Nov 1981), Maldives (9 Jul 1982), Saint Christopher and Nevis (19 Sep 1983), Brunei Darussalam (1 Jan 1984), Namibia (21 Mar 1990), Cameroon (13 Nov 1995), Mozambique (13 Nov 1995), Rwanda (29 Nov 2009)

Order for United Nations Events

The United Nations Flag

The United Nations Flag

The national flags of the United Nations members in order of their name as used at the UN. The exceptions to the normal alphabetical order are (with the sorting letter underlined):
Côte d'Ivoire (Ivory Coast), Democratic People's Republic of Korea (North Korea), Myanmar (Burma), Republic of Korea (South Korea), Republic of Moldova (Moldova), The Former Yugoslav Republic of Macedonia (Macedonia), Timor Leste (East Timor), United Republic of Tanzania (Tanzania)

Order for European Union Events

The European Union Flag

The European Union Flag

The national flags in order of their name in their primary local language. The local form is shown where its sorting letter differs from English:
Belgium, Bulgaria, Czech Republic, Denmark, *Deutschland* (Germany), *España* (Spain), Estonia, France, *Hellás* (Greece), Ireland, Italy, *Kypros* (Cyprus), Latvia, Lithuania, Luxembourg, *Magyarország* (Hungary), Malta, Netherlands, *Österreich* (Austria), Poland, Portugal, Romania, Slovakia, Slovenia, *Suomi* (Finland), Sweden, United Kingdom

English Alphabetical Order

To help with international flag displays the nations of the world are listed here in the normal English alphabetical order. The order uses the short name of the country rather than its formal name (ie. 'Australia' rather than 'Commonwealth of Australia') and ignores 'The'. Some of the names that might not be familiar are: Congo-Brazzaville - the former French colony of Congo; Congo-Kinshasa - the former Belgian Congo, now formally called the Democratic Republic of Congo; and Côte d'Ivoire - the Ivory Coast.

The countries marked with an asterix (*) are British (the constituent countries of the UK, the Crown Dependencies and the British Overseas Territories); for displays of flags within these countries, dependencies or territories, the local national flag takes precedence immediately after the Union Flag and before any British ensigns (White, RAF, Red, Blue and Civil Air). The remainder should be displayed in alphabetical order as shown, with the countries that make up the United Kingdom taking precedence.

Countries marked with a dagger symbol (†) are dependencies of other nations. Please note that the Taiwan flag may cause offence to representatives of the People's Republic of China.

United Kingdom
England*
Scotland*
Wales*
Alderney*
Anguilla*
Bermuda*
British Antarctic
   Territory*
British Indian Ocean
   Territory*
British Virgin Islands*
Cayman Islands*
Falkland Islands*
Gibraltar*
Guernsey*
Isle of Man*
Jersey*
Montserrat*
Pitcairn Islands*
Saint Helena*
Sark*
South Georgia and the
   South Sandwich Islands*
Tristan da Cunha*
Turks and Caicos Islands*
Afghanistan
Albania
Algeria
American Samoa†
Andorra
Angola
Antigua and Barbuda
Argentina
Armenia
Aruba†
Australia
Austria
Azerbaijan
Bahamas, The
Bahrain
Bangladesh
Barbados
Belarus
Belgium
Belize
Benin
Bhután
Bolivia
Bosnia and Herzegovina
Botswana
Brazil
Brunei Darusalam
Bulgaria
Burkina Faso
Burma
Burundi
Cambodia
Cameroon
Canada

Cape Verde
Central African Republic
Chad
Chile
China
Christmas Island†
Colombia
Comoros
Congo-Brazzaville
Congo-Kinshasa (DR)
Cook Islands†
Costa Rica
Côte d'Ivoire
Croatia
Cuba
Cyprus
Czech Republic
Denmark
Djibouti
Dominica
Dominican Republic
Ecuador
Egypt
El Salvador
Equatorial Guinea
Eritrea
Estonia
Ethiopia
Faroe Islands†
Fiji
Finland
France
French Polynesia†
Gabon
Gambia, The
Georgia
Germany
Ghana
Greece
Greenland†
Grenada
Guam†
Guatemala
Guinea
Guinea-Bissau
Guyana
Haiti
Honduras
Hong Kong SAR†
Hungary
Iceland
India
Indonesia
Irân
Iraq
Ireland
Israel
Italy
Jamaica
Japan

Jordan
Kazakhstan
Kenya
Kiribati
Kosovo
Kuwait
Kyrgyzstan
Laos
Latvia
Lebanon
Lesotho
Liberia
Libya
Liechtenstein
Lithuania
Luxembourg
Macau SAR†
Macedonia
Madagascar
Malawi
Malaysia
Maldives
Mali
Malta
Marshall Islands
Mauritania
Mauritius
México
Micronesia
Moldova
Monaco
Mongolia
Montenegro
Morocco
Mozambique
Namibia
Nauru
Nepal
Netherlands, The
Netherlands Antilles†
New Zealand
Nicaragua
Niger
Nigeria
Niue†
Norfolk Island†
North Korea
Northern Marianas†
Norway
Oman
Pakistan
Palau
Panamá
Papua New Guinea
Paraguay
Perú
Philippines
Poland
Portugal
Puerto Rico†

Qatar
România
Russian Federation
Rwanda
Saint Kitts and Nevis
Saint Lucia
Saint Vincent and
   the Grenadines
Samoa
San Marino
São Tomé and Príncipe
Saudi Arabia
Senegal
Serbia
Seychelles
Sierra Leone
Singapore
Slovakia
Slovenia
Solomon Islands
Somalia
South Africa
South Korea
Spain
Sri Lanka
Sudan
Suriname
Swaziland
Sweden
Switzerland
Syria
Taiwan
Tajikistan
Tanzania
Thailand
Timor Leste
Togo
Tokelau†
Tonga
Trinidad and Tobago
Tunisia
Turkey
Turkmenistan
Tuvalu
Uganda
Ukraine
United Arab Emirates
United States of America
Uruguay
Uzbekistan
Vanuatu
Vatican City
Venezuela
Viêt Nam
Virgin Islands†
Yemen
Zambia
Zimbabwe

Appendix C - United Kingdom Flag Specifications

The normal proportions for the national flags of the United Kingdom are 3:5 on land, but ensigns are customarily made in proportion 1:2.

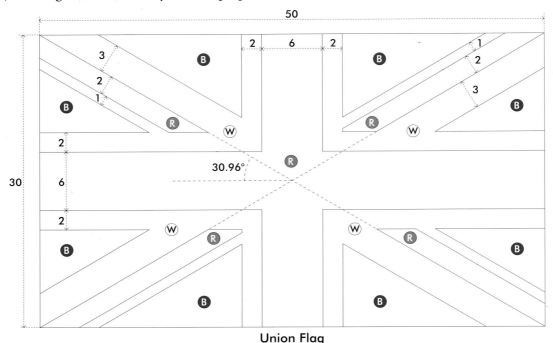

Union Flag

This is the 3:5 version for use on land. The specification for the 1:2 version replaces the length of 50 with 60 and the angle of 30.96° with 26.57°.

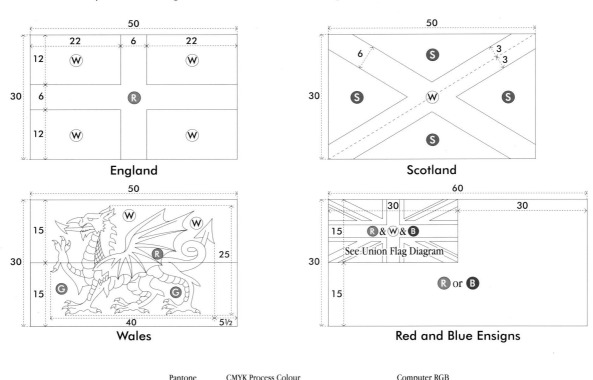

England

Scotland

Wales

Red and Blue Ensigns

Colour	Pantone Colour	CMYK Process Colour				Computer RGB		
		C	M	Y	K	R	G	B
B Royal Blue	280 C	100%	72%	0%	18.5%	0	36	125
R Red	186 C	0%	91%	76%	6%	207	20	43
W White	-	0%	0%	0%	0%	255	255	255
S Saltire Blue	300 C	100%	43%	0%	0%	0	110	199
G Green	354 C	91%	0%	83%	0%	0	176	82

Resource Book

Copyright © Scripture Union
First published 2015
ISBN 978 1 78506 331 2

British Library Cataloguing-in-Publication Data: a catalogue record of this book is available from the British Library.

Printed in Malta by Melita Press

Contributors: Dan Harris, Steve Hutchinson, Daniel Mosby, Lianne Semans Smith

Cover design and internal layout by Jake Howe

 Scripture Union is an international Christian charity working with churches in more than 130 countries.

Thank you for purchasing this resource. Any profits from this book support SU in England and Wales to bring the good news of Jesus Christ to children, young people and families and to enable them to meet God through the Bible and prayer.

Find out more about our work and how you can get involved at:
www.scriptureunion.org.uk (England and Wales)
www.suscotland.org.uk (Scotland)
www.suni.co.uk (Northern Ireland)
www.scriptureunion.org (USA)
www.su.org.au (Australia)

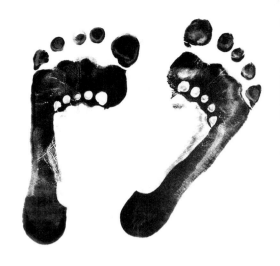

Contents

How to... Explore Together

Within our faith communities there is a rich diversity of God's people all at different stages in their faith development and spiritual experience, and all with different learning needs and preferences. We are a beautiful collection of artists, scholars, reflectors, dancers, data collectors, fact finders, readers, sculptors, writers, musicians, actors, talkers and listeners.

Explore Together places the Bible at the centre of this diversity. It is a new and practical tool for helping people to explore God's Word and hear his voice in a way that embraces their natural preferences. It encourages the community to come together to share their thoughts, questions and revelations with each other. Any and all are welcome and there are no barriers to participation.

At the heart of Explore Together is a desire to see people hear from God and learn more of his love for them. It works with big groups, small groups, mixed-age groups, single-age groups, older people, young people, children, families, house groups, church congregations, youth groups, school groups... in fact, Explore Together can be used in any environment with any group dynamic. It is grounded in years of research and tried and tested in a multitude of contexts.

This resource book is designed to equip you and your community as you adventure, journey and grow with God. On this page and the next we have a few suggestions on how to get the most out of the sessions in this resource and how to use the accompanying resources on the Explore Together website (www.exploretogether.org).

The green Explore Together resource book is also available, with another 12 sessions on a variety of themes.

The six steps

There are six essential steps to an Explore Together session, each of which can be tailored to slot into any existing structure and space:

1 **Prepare**
2 **Presenting the Bible**
3 **Pray**
4 **Explore**
5 **Share**
6 **Giving thanks**

These steps are explained in detail in each session outline.

Step 4 provides an opportunity for people to engage with God's Word using the Explore Together questions and the six Explore Together zones. Each zone has been carefully designed to cater for particular learning needs and preferences:

 Colour Zone – for those who learn by seeing

 Listening Zone – for those who learn by hearing

 Chat Zone – for those who learn by thinking aloud

 Word Zone – for those who learn by reading

 Busy Zone – for those who learn by doing

 Quiet Zone – for those who learn by reflecting

Individuals can choose to spend all of their exploring time in one zone, but may also choose to visit several zones, depending upon their preferences. There is no right or wrong amount of time to spend in a zone.

It is quite deliberate that no specific instructions are provided for each zone. Individuals are free to engage however they like with the resources provided in each area as they consider the Explore Together questions for the session.

Basic kit

Although every Explore Together session is different, there are some common elements that are always included. We will refer to these as the 'basic kit' for Explore Together. Before running your first session we advise that you acquire the following items, and top them up as required:

- Explore Together zone signs (available from www.exploretogether.org)
- Explore Together background soundtrack (available from www.exploretogether.org)
- MP3 players (or the means to play downloaded MP3 tracks – eg CDs and CD player)
- plasticine, play dough or clay
- plastic building bricks
- junk modelling items
- pipe cleaners
- pens, pencils and paper
- coloured pencils/pens
- coloured chalk sticks
- pastels/crayons
- glue
- scissors (child-safe)
- masking tape
- white paper
- black paper
- paper of different sorts, sizes and colours
- manuscript paper
- squared paper
- lined paper
- sticky notes
- a selection of Bible commentaries
- a selection of Bibles (different translations)
- children's Bibles and Bible story books, eg *The Big Bible Storybook* (Scripture Union, 2007)
- chairs/cushions/beanbags
- a separate area where people can be quiet

Each session will need a selection of other resources, detailed in Step 1. Many multimedia resources for each session are available for free from www.exploretogether.org/downloads (using the code from the bottom of page 32).

Gathering a team

Although it is entirely possible to lead an Explore Together session alone, it is much more effective when there is a team of people working together to share the responsibility and to model involvement. Strategically placed active participants will encourage others to participate.

The colour, word and busy zones benefit from having a carefully placed team member present to keep the focus on the questions, to engage in the zone activity and to draw people into the questions without dominating. The chat zone requires an experienced host to keep everyone focused.

For detailed team member role descriptions visit www.exploretogether.org.

FAQs

If you have any further questions, it's likely we've answered them in our FAQ section on pages 30 to 32 at the back of this book. If not, please don't hesitate to get in touch via the Scripture Union website: www.scriptureunion.org.uk.

If you'd like to know more about the ideas that underpin Explore Together and hear about our experiences of Explore Together in action, please read our companion book:

Explore Together: The Journey

You are mine

Matthew 3:16,17

Themes: acceptance, love, guidance, assurance, approval, baptism

This passage describes a defining moment in the life of Jesus before he starts his public ministry. At his baptism in the River Jordan, his Father affirms, approves and accepts him.

Prepare

Resources required

- 'John baptises Jesus' story text (from *The Big Bible Storybook*)
- 'John baptises Jesus' audio recording (from *The Big Bible Storybook* audio book)
- 'You are mine' image collection
- 'You are mine' word collection
- Matthew 3:16,17 (CEV)
- 'You are mine' Explore Together questions (PDF and PowerPoint)

All available from www.exploretogether.org/downloads (using the code from the bottom of page 32).

You will also need to gather:
- *You Are Mine* by Max Lucado (Candle Books, 2005)
- audio versions of different translations of Matthew 3:16,17
- various threads/ribbons with which to make bracelets
- Scratch Art doodle sheets
- items from the Explore Together basic kit (see page 5)

Presenting the Bible

With the community gathered together, begin by sharing the words from Matthew 3:16,17. Consider carefully which version of the Bible you choose to read from.

Alternatively or in addition you may choose to:
- read the whole or just a small portion of *You Are Mine* by Max Lucado (Candle Books, 2005)

Without being tempted to answer them, introduce the following questions to your community for them to consider:

- **What might God want you to notice in these verses?**
- **How did hearing these words change Jesus' life?**
- **How does it feel to know that God loves you just as much as he loves Jesus?**
- **What parts of your life do you think please God?**

Pray

Pray for and with your community, asking God to help you hear from him. This time of prayer can be creative, interactive, responsive, meditative or sung. It could also include communion and intercession. Ensure that there is a place set aside where people can go if they feel that they need someone to pray with them specifically. Have a small team of people available to offer prayer if required. Prayer ministry should be available throughout an Explore Together session.

You may like to use the prayer available on the website.

Explore

Read out your questions from Step 2 again or display them on a screen. Remind your community to consider these questions as they separate into their explore zones. Some may choose to consider all the questions while others may focus on just one. Some may completely ignore the questions and just open themselves up to God.

Invite your community to separate into small groups, around the zone(s) of their preference. Explain that individuals are welcome to spend as much or as little time in each zone as they wish, engaging at whatever level they feel comfortable. Depending upon where your quiet zone is located, you may wish to provide directions and remind people not to disturb one another when using this space.

Colour Zone
- crayons, pencils, pens
- paper of different sorts, sizes and colours
- 'You are mine' image collection
- Scratch Art doodle sheets
- copies of the 'You are mine' ET questions

Listening Zone
- 'John baptises Jesus' audio recording (from *The Big Bible Storybook* audio book)
- audio versions of different translations of Matthew 3:16,17
- someone to read aloud from *You Are Mine* by Max Lucado (Candle Books, 2005)
- copies of the 'You are mine' ET questions

Chat Zone
- a separate area with chairs, cushions or beanbags
- a chat zone host who is willing to read the passage again and then lead a discussion around the questions
- copies of Matthew 3:16,17 (CEV) or Bibles
- copies of the 'You are mine' ET questions

Word Zone
- pens, pencils, paper
- biblical commentaries relating to Matthew 3:16,17
- 'You are mine' word collection
- copies of *You Are Mine* by Max Lucado (Candle Books, 2005)
- 'John baptises Jesus' story text
- other children's Bibles and Bible story books containing a version of Matthew 3:16,17
- copies of Matthew 3:16,17 (CEV) or Bibles
- copies of the 'You are mine' ET questions

Busy Zone

- plasticine, play dough or clay
- pipe cleaners
- various threads/ribbons with which to make bracelets
- copies of the 'You are mine' ET questions

Quiet Zone

- a separate area where people can be alone with their thoughts and God
- 'You are mine' image collection (optional)
- copies of Matthew 3:16,17 (CEV) or Bibles
- copies of the 'You are mine' ET questions

Share

As your time for exploring together draws to a close, invite your community to come back together into small groups of three to five. Suggest that they share their responses to the questions posed at the beginning.

Giving thanks

Invite the explorers to share their reflections with the wider community, drawing together their responses and noting any common themes that emerge. Conclude by reading Matthew 3:16,17 (from the same Bible version used earlier). Then lead your community in a prayer, thanking God for all that he has revealed through this story. Encourage your community to continue their conversations about this story as they leave, and to take with them any artwork/writings/thoughts from the session.

Making disciples
Matthew 28:18–20

Themes: mission, purpose, power, local, global, evangelism

Within these final words of Matthew's Gospel we find a calling for every Christian to go and tell others of the good news, so that they too may encounter the love of God.

Prepare

Resources required
- 'Jesus is with us' story text (from *The Big Bible Storybook*)
- 'The good news' poem text
- 'The good news' poem audio recording
- 'Jesus is with us' audio recording (from *The Big Bible Storybook* audio book)
- 'Making disciples' image collection
- 'Making disciples' word collection
- Matthew 28:18–20 (CEV)
- 'Making disciples' Explore Together questions (PDF and PowerPoint)

All available from www.exploretogether.org/downloads (using the code from the bottom of page 32).

You will also need to gather:
- old magazines to cut up (with inappropriate content removed)
- paints, brushes and appropriate table coverings
- audio versions of different translations of Matthew 28:18–20
- literature from local, national or global mission, discipleship and evangelism agencies
- threads and various collections of beads
- small mirrors, tissues and wipe-clean whiteboard markers
- items from the Explore Together basic kit (see page 5)
- someone involved in local, national or global mission activity who is willing to share a little about their ministry (optional)

Presenting the Bible

With the community gathered together, begin by sharing the words from Matthew 28:18–20. Consider carefully which version of the Bible you choose to read from.

Alternatively or in addition you may choose to:
- invite members of your church or community who are involved in mission activity locally, nationally or globally to share a little of their work, but also their motivation for this kind of ministry

Without being tempted to answer them, introduce the following questions to your community for them to consider:

- **What does this story tell you about God?**
- **Who are the people you want to tell about Jesus?**
- **What is the good news?**
- **What do you need from God to help you share his good news?**

Pray

Pray for and with your community, asking God to help you hear from him. This time of prayer can be creative, interactive, responsive, meditative or sung. It could also include communion and intercession. Ensure that there is a place set aside where people can go if they feel that they need someone to pray with them specifically. Have a small team of people available to offer prayer if required. Prayer ministry should be available throughout an Explore Together session.

If you invited those involved in mission activity to share earlier, you might like to take this opportunity to pray for them and their ministry.

Explore

Read out your questions from Step 2 again or display them on a screen. Remind your community to consider these questions as they separate into their explore zones. Some may choose to consider all the questions while others may focus on just one. Some may completely ignore the questions and just open themselves up to God.

Invite your community to separate into small groups, around the zone(s) of their preference. Explain that individuals are welcome to spend as much or as little time in each zone as they wish, engaging at whatever level they feel comfortable. Depending upon where your quiet zone is located, you may wish to provide directions and remind people not to disturb one another when using this space.

Colour Zone

- white paper in various sizes
- scissors
- glue
- 'Making disciples' image collection
- old magazines to cut up
- paint, brushes and appropriate table coverings
- copies of the 'Making disciples' ET questions

Listening Zone

- 'Jesus is with us' audio recording (from *The Big Bible Storybook* audio book)
- audio versions of different translations of Matthew 28:18–20
- 'The good news' poem audio recording
- someone involved in local, national or global mission activity to share a little about their ministry (optional)
- copies of the 'Making disciples' ET questions

Chat Zone

- a separate area with chairs, cushions or beanbags
- a chat zone host who is willing to read the passage again and then lead a discussion around the questions
- someone involved in local, national or global mission activity to share a little about their ministry (optional)
- copies of Matthew 28:18–20 (CEV) or Bibles
- copies of the 'Making disciples' ET questions

Word Zone

- pens, pencils, paper
- biblical commentaries relating to Matthew 28:18–20
- 'Making disciples' word collection
- 'Jesus is with us' story text
- other children's Bibles and Bible story books containing a version of Matthew 28:18–20
- copies of Matthew 28:18–20 (CEV) or Bibles
- literature from local, national or global mission, discipleship and evangelism agencies
- copies of 'The good news' poem text
- copies of the 'Making disciples' ET questions

Busy Zone
- pipe cleaners
- junk modelling items
- threads and various collections of beads
- small mirrors, tissues and wipe-clean whiteboard markers
- copies of the 'Making disciples' ET questions

Quiet Zone
- a separate area where people can be alone with their thoughts and God
- 'Making disciples' image collection (optional)
- copies of Matthew 28:18–20 (CEV) or Bibles
- copies of the 'Making disciples' ET questions

Share

As your time for exploring together draws to a close, invite your community to come back together into small groups of three to five. Suggest that they share their responses to the questions posed at the beginning.

Giving thanks

Invite the explorers to share their reflections with the wider community, drawing together their responses and noting any common themes that emerge. Conclude by reading Matthew 28:18–20 again (from the same Bible version used earlier). Then lead your community in a prayer, thanking God for all that he has revealed through this story. Alternatively, use the closing activity from the website. Encourage your community to continue their conversations about this story as they leave, and to take with them any artwork/writings/thoughts from the session.

The greatest command

Mark 12:30,31

Themes: love, other people, the kingdom of God, sacrifice, challenge

When asked which of the commandments was the greatest, Jesus managed to sum up the whole of the Old Testament Law in just two new commands – forming a significant part of the bedrock and foundation of the Christian faith.

Prepare

Resources required
- 'Love' image collection
- 'Love' word collection
- Mark 12:30,31 (CEV)
- 'Love' Explore Together questions (PDF and PowerPoint)

All available from www.exploretogether.org/downloads (using the code from the bottom of page 32).

You will also need to gather:
- audio recordings of different translations of Mark 12:30,31
- paints, paintbrushes, appropriate table coverings etc
- copies of *The Lion Handbook to the Bible* or similar Bible dictionaries
- loom bands
- threads and various collections of beads
- items from the Explore Together basic kit (see page 5)
- someone to deliver a short sermon (optional)

Presenting the Bible

With the community gathered together, begin by sharing the words from Mark 12:30,31. Consider carefully which version of the Bible you choose to read from.

Alternatively or in addition you may choose to use one of the following:
- ask for a group of volunteers to read the passage together, one word or phrase at a time
- present the reading using alternative media alongside, such as video, photography, dance or art

Without being tempted to answer them, introduce the following questions to your community for them to consider:

- **What is God saying to you through these verses?**
- **How does loving God like this affect your daily life?**
- **Is there a difference between the type of love Jesus mentions and the human kind of love?**
- **How would your community change if this kind of love was put into practice?**

Pray

Pray for and with your community, asking God to help you hear from him. This time of prayer can be creative, interactive, responsive, meditative or sung. It could also include communion and intercession. Ensure that there is a place set aside where people can go if they feel that they need someone to pray with them specifically. Have a small team of people available to offer prayer if required. Prayer ministry should be available throughout an Explore Together session.

Explore

Read out your questions from Step 2 again or display them on a screen. Remind your community to consider these questions as they separate into their explore zones. Some may choose to consider all the questions while others may focus on just one. Some may completely ignore the questions and just open themselves up to God.

Invite your community to separate into small groups, around the zone(s) of their preference. Explain that individuals are welcome to spend as much or as little time in each zone as they wish, engaging at whatever level they feel comfortable. Depending upon where your quiet zone is located, you may wish to provide directions and remind people not to disturb one another when using this space.

Colour Zone

- crayons, coloured pens, white and coloured paper
- paints, paintbrushes, appropriate table coverings etc
- 'Love' image collection
- copies of the 'Love' ET questions

Listening Zone

- audio recordings of different translations of Mark 12:30,31
- copies of the 'Love' ET questions
- you may wish to deliver a short sermon in this zone

Chat Zone

- a separate area with chairs, cushions or beanbags
- a chat zone host who is willing to read the passage again and then lead a discussion around the questions
- copies of Mark 12:30,31 (CEV) or Bibles
- copies of the 'Love' ET questions

Word Zone

- pens, pencils, paper
- biblical commentaries relating to Mark 12:30,31
- 'Love' word collection
- Bible story books containing a version of Mark 12:30,31
- copies of Mark 12:30,31 (CEV) or Bibles
- copies of *The Lion Handbook to the Bible* or similar Bible dictionaries
- copies of the 'Love' ET questions

Busy Zone

- plastic building bricks
- plasticine, play dough or clay
- loom bands
- threads and various collections of beads
- copies of the 'Love' ET questions

Quiet Zone

- a separate area where people can be alone with their thoughts and God
- 'Love' image collection (optional)
- copies of Mark 12:30,31 (CEV) or Bibles
- copies of the 'Love' ET questions

Share

As your time for exploring together draws to a close, invite your community to come back together into small groups of three to five. Suggest that they share their responses to the questions posed at the beginning.

Giving thanks

Invite the explorers to share their reflections with the wider community, drawing together their responses and noting any common themes that emerge. Conclude by reading Mark 12:30,31 again (from the same Bible version used earlier). Then lead your community in a prayer, thanking God for all that he has revealed through this story. Encourage your community to continue their conversations about this story as they leave, and to take with them any artwork/writings/thoughts from the session.

Firm foundations

Luke 6:46–49   Themes: foundations, building, listening, obedience, commitment, strength

Building a house on rock would have required significantly more effort and commitment than a house on sand. Our relationship with God is sometimes hard work, but it's always worth it!

Prepare

Resources required
- 'Jesus the storyteller' audio recording (from *The Big Bible Storybook* audio book)
- 'Firm foundations' image collection
- 'Firm foundations' word collection
- Luke 6:46–49 (CEV)
- 'Firm foundations' Explore Together questions (PDF and PowerPoint)

All available from www.exploretogether.org/downloads (using the code from the bottom of page 32).

You will also need to gather:
- flags and ribbons
- 'The wise man built his house upon the rock' song (various versions available at www.itunes.com)
- notebooks
- a tray of play sand
- large pebbles
- fairy lights (optional)
- items from the Explore Together basic kit (see page 5)
- someone to deliver a short sermon on Luke 6:46–49 (optional)

Presenting the Bible

With the community gathered together, begin by sharing the words from Luke 6:46–49. Consider carefully which version of the Bible you choose to read from.

Without being tempted to answer them, introduce the following questions to your community for them to consider:

- **What strikes you about this passage?**
- **What foundations are you building your life upon?**
- **How firm are your foundations?**
- **How might you need to change your foundations?**

Pray

Pray for and with your community, asking God to help you hear from him. This time of prayer can be creative, interactive, responsive, meditative or sung. It could also include communion and intercession. Ensure that there is a place set aside where people can go if they feel that they need someone to pray with them specifically. Have a small team of people available to offer prayer if required. Prayer ministry should be available throughout an Explore Together session.

Explore

Read out your questions from Step 2 again or display them on a screen. Remind your community to consider these questions as they separate into their explore zones. Some may choose to consider all the questions while others may focus on just one. Some may completely ignore the questions and just open themselves up to God.

Invite your community to separate into small groups, around the zone(s) of their preference. Explain that individuals are welcome to spend as much or as little time in each zone as they wish, engaging at whatever level they feel comfortable. Depending upon where your quiet zone is located, you may wish to provide directions and remind people not to disturb one another when using this space.

Colour Zone
- pens and pencils
- crayons
- large sheets of white paper
- coloured paper of various sizes
- flags and ribbons
- 'Firm foundations' image collection
- copies of the 'Firm foundations' ET questions

Listening Zone
- MP3 players with a version of 'The wise man built his house upon the rock' song
- 'Jesus the storyteller' audio recording (from *The Big Bible Storybook* audio book)
- audio versions of different translations of Luke 6:46–49
- someone to deliver a short sermon on this passage (optional)
- copies of the 'Firm foundations' ET questions

Chat Zone
- a separate area with chairs, cushions or beanbags
- a chat zone host who is willing to read the passage again and then lead a discussion around the questions
- copies of Luke 6:46–49 (CEV) or Bibles
- copies of the 'Firm foundations' ET questions

Word Zone
- pens, pencils, paper
- squared paper and notebooks
- biblical commentaries relating to Luke 6:46–49
- 'Firm foundations' word collection
- copies of *The Big Bible Storybook* open at 'Jesus the storyteller', or other children's Bibles and Bible story books containing a version of Luke 6:46–49
- copies of Luke 6:46–49 (CEV) or Bibles
- copies of the 'Firm foundations' ET questions

Busy Zone
- plastic building bricks
- plasticine, play dough or clay
- a tray of play sand
- large pebbles
- copies of the 'Firm foundations' ET questions

Quiet Zone
- a separate area where people can be alone with their thoughts and God
- 'Firm foundations' image collection (optional)
- fairy lights (optional)
- copies of Luke 6:46–49 (CEV) or Bibles
- copies of the 'Firm foundations' ET questions

Share

As your time for exploring together draws to a close, invite your community to come back together into small groups of three to five. Suggest that they share their responses to the questions posed at the beginning.

Giving thanks

Invite the explorers to share their reflections with the wider community, drawing together their responses and noting any common themes that emerge. Conclude by reading Luke 6:46–49 again (from the same Bible version used earlier). Then lead your community in a prayer, thanking God for all that he has revealed through this story. Encourage your community to continue their conversations about this story as they leave, and to take with them any artwork/writings/thoughts from the session.

Healing and wholeness

Luke 8:40–56

Themes: healing, faith, trust, illness, grief, pain, God's power

All of us will encounter significant illness at some point, whether it is in our own life or in the lives of those close to us – it is an everyday reality. In this story, Jesus reminds us of God's power and presence in the face of illness.

Prepare

Resources required
- 'Healing and wholeness' deeper study
- 'Where are you Lord?' audio meditation and PDF
- 'Barely touching' image
- 'Healing and wholeness' reflection audio recording
- 'Jairus and his daughter' story text (from *The Big Bible Storybook*)
- 'Jairus and his daughter' audio recording (from *The Big Bible Storybook* audio book)
- 'Healing and wholeness' image collection
- 'Healing and wholeness' word collection
- Luke 8:40–56 (CEV)
- 'Healing and wholeness' Explore Together questions (PDF and PowerPoint)

You will also need to gather:
- a copy of *The Miracle Maker* DVD (2000, Icon Home Entertainment) (optional)
- audio versions of different translations of Luke 8:40–56
- cushions and blankets
- items from the Explore Together basic kit (see page 5)

All available from www.exploretogether.org/downloads (using the code from the bottom of page 32).

Presenting the Bible

With the community gathered together, begin by sharing the words from Luke 8:40–56. Consider carefully which version of the Bible you choose to read from.

Alternatively or in addition you may choose to do the following:
- watch a clip from *The Miracle Maker* DVD showing the events in today's story.

Without being tempted to answer them, introduce the following questions to your community for them to consider:

- **What makes it difficult for you to get close to Jesus?**
- **Who are you most like in this story, and why?**
- **In what ways can we get close to Jesus?**
- **If Jesus asked you today, 'What can I do for you?', what would you say?**

Pray

Pray for and with your community, asking God to help you hear from him. This time of prayer can be creative, interactive, responsive, meditative or sung. It could also include communion and intercession. Ensure that there is a place set aside where people can go if they feel that they need someone to pray with them specifically. Have a small team of people available to offer prayer if required. Prayer ministry should be available throughout an Explore Together session.

Explore

Read out your questions from Step 2 again or display them on a screen. Remind your community to consider these questions as they separate into their explore zones. Some may choose to consider all the questions while others may focus on just one. Some may completely ignore the questions and just open themselves up to God.

Invite your community to separate into small groups, around the zone(s) of their preference. Explain that individuals are welcome to spend as much or as little time in each zone as they wish, engaging at whatever level they feel comfortable. Depending upon where your quiet zone is located, you may wish to provide directions and remind people not to disturb one another when using this space.

Colour Zone
- coloured pencils and crayons
- paper of different colours and sizes
- glue
- scissors
- chalk and black paper
- copies of the 'Healing and wholeness' ET questions

Listening Zone
- MP3 players with the 'Where are you Lord?' audio meditation and 'Healing and wholeness' reflection on them
- 'Jairus and his daughter' audio recording (from *The Big Bible Storybook* audio book)
- audio versions of different translations of Luke 8:40–56
- a selection of Bible story books containing a version of Luke 8:40–56 to read with small children
- cushions and blankets

Chat Zone
- a separate area with chairs, cushions or beanbags
- a chat zone host who is willing to read the passage again and then lead a discussion around the questions
- copies of Luke 8:40–56 (CEV) or Bibles
- copies of the 'Healing and wholeness' ET questions

Word Zone

- pens, pencils, paper
- biblical commentaries relating to Luke 8:40–56
- 'Healing and wholeness' word collection
- copies of *The Big Bible Storybook* open at 'Jairus and his daughter', or other children's Bibles and Bible story books containing a version of Luke 8:40–56
- copies of Luke 8:40–56 (CEV) or Bibles
- copies of the 'Healing and wholeness' ET questions

Busy Zone
- pipe cleaners
- plasticine, play dough or clay
- junk modelling items
- masking tape
- scissors
- copies of the 'Healing and wholeness' ET questions

Quiet Zone
- a separate area where people can be alone with their thoughts and God
- 'Healing and wholeness' image collection (optional)
- copies of Luke 8:40–56 (CEV) or Bibles
- copies of the 'Healing and wholeness' ET questions

Share

As your time for exploring together draws to a close, invite your community to come back together into small groups of three to five. Suggest that they share their responses to the questions posed at the beginning.

Giving thanks

Invite the explorers to share their reflections with the wider community, drawing together their responses and noting any common themes that emerge. Conclude by reading Luke 8:40–56 again (from the same Bible version used earlier). Then lead your community in a prayer, thanking God for all that he has revealed through this story. Encourage your community to continue their conversations about this story as they leave, and to take with them any artwork/writings/thoughts from the session.

Lessons in prayer

Luke 11:1–13

Themes: forgiveness, provision, instruction, guidance, prayer, relationship

The Lord's Prayer may well be very familiar to you, but be careful to remember that this prayer is rooted deeply in the power and glory of God. No matter how many times we return to a well-known Bible passage, God always has something new to teach us.

Prepare

Resources required
- 'Jesus' prayer' story text (from *The Big Bible Storybook*)
- 'Jesus' prayer' audio recording (from *The Big Bible Storybook* audio book)
- 'Lessons in prayer' image collection
- 'Lessons in prayer' word collection
- Luke 11:1–13 (CEV)
- 'Lessons in prayer' Explore Together questions (PDF and PowerPoint)

All available from www.exploretogether.org/downloads (using the code from the bottom of page 32).

You will also need to gather:
- a copy of *The Jesus Storybook Bible* by Sally Lloyd-Jones (Zondervan, 2012) (optional)
- audio versions of different translations of Luke 11:1–13
- coloured matchsticks
- beads and string for threading
- play sand in trays with plastic spoons and yoghurt pots
- items from the Explore Together basic kit (see page 5)
- someone to deliver a short sermon on the theme of prayer (optional)

Presenting the Bible

With the community gathered together, begin by sharing the words from Luke 11:1–13. Consider carefully which version of the Bible you choose to read from.

Alternatively or in addition you may choose to use the following:
- 'How to pray' from *The Jesus Storybook Bible* by Sally Lloyd-Jones (Zondervan, 2012)

Without being tempted to answer them, introduce the following questions to your community for them to consider:

- **How does hearing Jesus' teaching on prayer make you feel?**
- **Why are his words important for us today?**
- **How has prayer deepened your relationship with God?**
- **What do you want to say to God now?**

Pray

Pray for and with your community, asking God to help you hear from him. This time of prayer can be creative, interactive, responsive, meditative or sung. It could also include communion and intercession. Ensure that there is a place set aside where people can go if they feel that they need someone to pray with them specifically. Have a small team of people available to offer prayer if required. Prayer ministry should be available throughout an Explore Together session.

Explore

Read out your questions from Step 2 again or display them on a screen. Remind your community to consider these questions as they separate into their explore zones. Some may choose to consider all the questions while others may focus on just one. Some may completely ignore the questions and just open themselves up to God.

Invite your community to separate into small groups, around the zone(s) of their preference. Explain that individuals are welcome to spend as much or as little time in each zone as they wish, engaging at whatever level they feel comfortable. Depending upon where your quiet zone is located, you may wish to provide directions and remind people not to disturb one another when using this space.

Colour Zone
- coloured pencils and crayons
- paper of different colours and sizes
- coloured matchsticks
- glue
- 'Lessons in prayer' image collection
- copies of the 'Lessons in prayer' ET questions

Listening Zone
- 'Jesus' prayer' audio recording (from *The Big Bible Storybook* audio book)
- audio versions of different translations of Luke 11:1–13
- someone to deliver a short sermon on the theme of prayer (optional)
- copies of the 'Lessons in prayer' ET questions

Chat Zone
- a separate area with chairs, cushions or beanbags
- a chat zone host who is willing to read the passage again and then lead a discussion around the questions
- copies of Luke 11:1–13 (CEV) or Bibles
- copies of the 'Lessons in prayer' ET questions

Word Zone
- pens, pencils, paper
- biblical commentaries relating to Luke 11:1–13
- 'Lessons in prayer' word collection
- copies of *The Big Bible Storybook* open at 'Jesus' prayer', or other children's Bibles and Bible story books containing a version of Luke 11:1–13
- copies of Luke 11:1–13 (CEV) or Bibles
- copies of the 'Lessons in prayer' ET questions

Busy Zone
- plasticine, play dough or clay
- plastic building bricks
- beads and string for threading
- play sand in trays with plastic spoons and yoghurt pots
- copies of the 'Lessons in prayer' ET questions

Quiet Zone
- a separate area where people can be alone with their thoughts and God
- 'Lessons in prayer' image collection (optional)
- copies of Luke 11:1–13 (CEV) or Bibles
- copies of the 'Lessons in prayer' ET questions

Share

As your time for exploring together draws to a close, invite your community to come back together into small groups of three to five. Suggest that they share their responses to the questions posed at the beginning.

Giving thanks

Invite the explorers to share their reflections with the wider community, drawing together their responses and noting any common themes that emerge. Conclude by reading Luke 11:1–13 again (from the same Bible version used earlier). Then lead your community in a prayer, thanking God for all that he has revealed through this story. Encourage your community to continue their conversations about this story as they leave, and to take with them any artwork/writings/thoughts from the session.

Lost and found

Luke 15:1–7

Themes: unconditional love, care, security, forgiveness, celebration, belonging

The love of Jesus is bigger, better, wider and deeper than we could ever hope or imagine. Jesus searches for those who are lost and he seeks to draw them into his loving arms.

Prepare

Resources required
- 'The lost sheep' story text (from *The Big Bible Storybook*)
- 'The lost sheep' audio recording (from *The Big Bible Storybook* audio book)
- 'Lost and found' image collection
- 'Lost and found' word collection
- Luke 15:1–7 (CEV)
- 'Lost and found' Explore Together questions (PDF and PowerPoint)

All available from www.exploretogether.org/downloads (using the code from the bottom of page 32).

You will also need to gather:
- 'Cecil the Lost Sheep' storytelling kit available from www.lostsheep.com.au (optional)
- lengths of lining paper
- large paintbrushes
- paint in trays
- paper plates
- cotton wool
- pre-tangled lengths of wool (for untangling)
- audio versions of different translations of Luke 15:1–7
- copies of *The Lost Sheep* board book (Scripture Union, 2009) (optional)
- items from the Explore Together basic kit (see page 5)
- someone who is willing to share their testimony

Presenting the Bible

With the community gathered together, begin by sharing the words from Luke 15:1–7. Consider carefully which version of the Bible you choose to read from.

Alternatively you may choose to use the following resource to tell the story:
- 'Cecil the Lost Sheep' storytelling kit

Without being tempted to answer them, introduce the following questions to your community for them to consider:

- **What does this story teach us about the love of God?**
- **Why does Jesus want us to hear this story today?**
- **What part can you play in searching for the lost?**
- **What is God saying to you now?**

Pray

Pray for and with your community, asking God to help you hear from him. This time of prayer can be creative, interactive, responsive, meditative or sung. It could also include communion and intercession. Ensure that there is a place set aside where people can go if they feel that they need someone to pray with them specifically. Have a small team of people available to offer prayer if required. Prayer ministry should be available throughout an Explore Together session.

Explore

Read out your questions from Step 2 again or display them on a screen. Remind your community to consider these questions as they separate into their explore zones. Some may choose to consider all the questions while others may focus on just one. Some may completely ignore the questions and just open themselves up to God.

Invite your community to separate into small groups, around the zone(s) of their preference. Explain that individuals are welcome to spend as much or as little time in each zone as they wish, engaging at whatever level they feel comfortable. Depending upon where your quiet zone is located, you may wish to provide directions and remind people not to disturb one another when using this space.

Colour Zone
- coloured pencils and crayons
- coloured pens
- lengths of lining paper
- large paintbrushes
- paint in trays
- paper plates
- 'Lost and found' image collection
- copies of the 'Lost and found' ET questions

Listening Zone
- 'The lost sheep' audio recording (from *The Big Bible Storybook* audio book)
- audio versions of different translations of Luke 15:1–7
- copies of the 'Lost and found' ET questions
- someone who is willing to share their testimony

Chat Zone
- a separate area with chairs, cushions or beanbags
- a chat zone host who is willing to read the passage again and then lead a discussion around the questions
- copies of Luke 15:1–7 (CEV) or Bibles
- copies of the 'Lost and found' ET questions

Word Zone

- pens, pencils, paper
- sticky notes
- biblical commentaries relating to Luke 15:1–7
- 'Lost and found' word collection
- copies of *The Lost Sheep* board book (Scripture Union, 2009) or other children's Bibles and Bible story books containing a version of Luke 15:1–7
- copies of Luke 15:1–7 (CEV) or Bibles
- copies of the 'Lost and found' ET questions

Busy Zone
- items for junk modelling
- masking tape
- scissors
- glue
- pipe cleaners
- plasticine, play dough or clay
- cotton wool
- pre-tangled lengths of wool (for untangling)
- copies of the 'Lost and found' ET questions

Quiet Zone
- a separate area where people can be alone with their thoughts and God
- 'Lost and found' image collection (optional)
- copies of Luke 15:1–7 (CEV) or Bibles
- copies of the 'Lost and found' ET questions

Share

As your time for exploring together draws to a close, invite your community to come back together into small groups of three to five. Suggest that they share their responses to the questions posed at the beginning.

Giving thanks

Invite the explorers to share their reflections with the wider community, drawing together their responses and noting any common themes that emerge. Conclude by reading Luke 15:1–7 again (from the same Bible version used earlier). Then lead your community in a prayer, thanking God for all that he has revealed through this story. Encourage your community to continue their conversations about this story as they leave, and to take with them any artwork/writings/thoughts from the session.

A loving father

Luke 15:11–32

Themes: acceptance, repentance, unconditional love, restoration

When the religious leaders of the day (the Pharisees and scribes) accused Jesus of being friendly with sinners, he told them this parable to illustrate his Father's heart of love for all.

Prepare

Resources required
- 'A loving father' audio recording (from *The Big Bible Storybook* audio book)
- 'Father?' poem
- 'A loving father' image collection
- 'A loving father' word collection
- Luke 15:11–32 (CEV)
- 'A loving father' Explore Together questions (PDF and PowerPoint)

All available from www.exploretogether.org/downloads (using the code from the bottom of page 32).

You will also need to gather:
- audio versions of different translations of Luke 15:11–32
- copies of *The Loving Father* board book (Scripture Union, 2012) (optional)
- heart-shaped pieces of paper or heart-shaped stickers
- 'The father's love' by KXC (available from www. itunes.com)
- items from the Explore Together basic kit (see page 5)

Presenting the Bible

With the community gathered together, begin by sharing the words from Luke 15:11–32. Consider carefully which version of the Bible you choose to read from.

Without being tempted to answer them, introduce the following questions to your community for them to consider:

- **What is God saying to you through these verses?**
- **What does this passage tell you about God as Father?**
- **Which character in the passage do you relate to, and why?**
- **How have you experienced acceptance from God?**

Pray

Pray for and with your community, asking God to help you hear from him. This time of prayer can be creative, interactive, responsive, meditative or sung. It could also include communion and intercession. Ensure that there is a place set aside where people can go if they feel that they need someone to pray with them specifically. Have a small team of people available to offer prayer if required. Prayer ministry should be available throughout an Explore Together session.

Explore

Read out your questions from Step 2 again or display them on a screen. Remind your community to consider these questions as they separate into their explore zones. Some may choose to consider all the questions while others may focus on just one. Some may completely ignore the questions and just open themselves up to God.

Invite your community to separate into small groups, around the zone(s) of their preference. Explain that individuals are welcome to spend as much or as little time in each zone as they wish, engaging at whatever level they feel comfortable. Depending upon where your quiet zone is located, you may wish to provide directions and remind people not to disturb one another when using this space.

Colour Zone
- coloured chalk sticks
- black and white paper
- pastels/crayons
- glue
- 'A loving father' image collection
- heart-shaped pieces of paper or heart-shaped stickers
- copies of the 'A loving father' ET questions

Listening Zone
- 'A loving father' audio recording (from *The Big Bible Storybook* audio book)
- audio versions of different translations of Luke 15:11–32
- MP3 players with 'The father's love' audio
- copies of the 'A loving father' ET questions

Chat Zone
- a separate area with chairs, cushions or beanbags
- a chat zone host who is willing to read the passage again and then lead a discussion around the questions
- copies of Luke 15:11–32 (CEV) or Bibles
- copies of the 'A loving father' ET questions

Word Zone

- pens, pencils, paper
- biblical commentaries relating to Luke 15:11–32
- 'A loving father' word collection
- copies of *The Loving Father* board book (Scripture Union, 2012), or other children's Bibles and Bible story books containing a version of Luke 15:11–32
- copies of Luke 15:11–32 (CEV) or Bibles
- copies of the 'Father?' poem
- copies of the 'A loving father' ET questions

Busy Zone

- junk modelling items
- plasticine, play dough or clay
- masking tape, glue, scissors
- plastic building bricks
- copies of the 'A loving father' ET questions

Quiet Zone
- a separate area where people can be alone with their thoughts and God
- 'A loving father' image collection (optional)
- copies of Luke 15:11–32 (CEV) or Bibles
- copies of the 'A loving father' ET questions

Share

As your time for exploring together draws to a close, invite your community to come back together into small groups of three to five. Suggest that they share their responses to the questions posed at the beginning.

Giving thanks

Invite the explorers to share their reflections with the wider community, drawing together their responses and noting any common themes that emerge. Conclude by reading 15:11–32 again (from the same Bible version used earlier). Then lead your community in a prayer, thanking God for all that he has revealed through this story. Encourage your community to continue their conversations about this story as they leave, and to take with them any artwork/writings/thoughts from the session.

Honouring God

1 Corinthians 10:31

Themes: honouring God, worship, praise, lifestyle, commitment, discipleship

In writing this letter to the church in Corinth, Paul urges them to consider every aspect of their lives in the light of their commitment to Christ. The call for us to do the same is just as strong today.

Prepare

Resources required

- 'Honouring God' image collection
- 'Honouring God' word collection
- 1 Corinthians 10:31 (CEV)
- 'Honouring God' Explore Together questions (PDF and PowerPoint)

All available from www.exploretogether.org/downloads (using the code from the bottom of page 32).

You will also need to gather:

- 'Living for your glory' by Tim Hughes (various versions available from www.itunes.com)
- audio versions of different translations of 1 Corinthians 10:31
- sheets of card
- straws
- holding crosses (available from most Christian bookshops or online)
- items from the Explore Together basic kit (see page 5)

Presenting the Bible

With the community gathered together, begin by sharing the words from 1 Corinthians 10:31. Consider carefully which version of the Bible you choose to read from.

Alternatively or in addition you may choose to use the following:
- read a lengthier passage from the Bible, putting this single verse into a broader context; however, the remainder of this session will focus specifically on verse 31

Without being tempted to answer them, introduce the following questions to your community for them to consider:

- **What might God want to say to you today?**
- **What do you want to say to God?**
- **What does it mean to honour God?**
- **How can we honour God in everything?**

Pray

Pray for and with your community, asking God to help you hear from him. This time of prayer can be creative, interactive, responsive, meditative or sung. It could also include communion and intercession. Ensure that there is a place set aside where people can go if they feel that they need someone to pray with them specifically. Have a small team of people available to offer prayer if required. Prayer ministry should be available throughout an Explore Together session.

Explore

Read out your questions from Step 2 again or display them on a screen. Remind your community to consider these questions as they separate into their explore zones. Some may choose to consider all the questions while others may focus on just one. Some may completely ignore the questions and just open themselves up to God.

Invite your community to separate into small groups, around the zone(s) of their preference. Explain that individuals are welcome to spend as much or as little time in each zone as they wish, engaging at whatever level they feel comfortable. Depending upon where your quiet zone is located, you may wish to provide directions and remind people not to disturb one another when using this space.

Colour Zone
- pens, pencils, pastels and crayons
- sticks of chalk
- black paper
- white paper
- 'Honouring God' image collection
- copies of the 'Honouring God' ET questions

Listening Zone
- MP3 players with the song 'Living for your glory' by Tim Hughes
- audio versions of different translations of 1 Corinthians 10:31
- copies of the 'Honouring God' ET questions

Chat Zone
- a separate area with chairs, cushions or beanbags
- a chat zone host who is willing to read the passage again and then lead a discussion around the questions
- copies of 1 Corinthians 10:31 (CEV) or Bibles
- copies of the 'Honouring God' ET questions

Word Zone
- pens, pencils, paper
- biblical commentaries relating to 1 Corinthians 10:31
- 'Honouring God' word collection
- children's Bibles and Bible story books containing a version of 1 Corinthians 10:31
- copies of 1 Corinthians 10:31 (CEV) or Bibles
- copies of the 'Honouring God' ET questionss

Busy Zone
- plasticine, play dough or clay
- pipe cleaners
- plastic building bricks
- straws
- sheets of card
- glue
- scissors
- masking tape
- copies of the 'Honouring God' ET questions

Quiet Zone
- a separate area where people can be alone with their thoughts and God
- holding crosses
- 'Honouring God' image collection (optional)
- copies of 1 Corinthians 10:31 (CEV) or Bibles
- copies of the 'Honouring God' ET questions

Share

As your time for exploring together draws to a close, invite your community to come back together into small groups of three to five. Suggest that they share their responses to the questions posed at the beginning.

Giving thanks

Invite the explorers to share their reflections with the wider community, drawing together their responses and noting any common themes that emerge. Conclude by reading 1 Corinthians 10:31 again (from the same Bible version used earlier). Then lead your community in a prayer, thanking God for all that he has revealed through this story. Encourage your community to continue their conversations about this story as they leave, and to take with them any artwork/writings/thoughts from the session.

The fruit of the Spirit

Galatians 5:17–26

Themes: commitment, discipleship, integrity

Paul was a skilled tent maker; through his trade and the relationships he developed while working he was able to share his faith in a way that drew others into a relationship with God. Every day, every circumstance, every conversation was an opportunity for Paul to honour God – it should be the same for us. In his letter to the Colossians, Paul outlines a strategy to help us live for God day by day. These Bible passages demonstrate how being a follower of Jesus is a full-time commitment.

Prepare

Resources required
- 'The fruit of the Spirit' image collection
- 'The fruit of the Spirit' word collection
- Galatians 5:17–26 (CEV)
- 'The fruit of the Spirit' Explore Together questions (PDF and PowerPoint)

All available from www.exploretogether.org/downloads (using the code from the bottom of page 32).

You will also need to gather:
- many different coloured pieces of fabric
- audio versions of different translations of Galatians 5:17–26
- 'Open the eyes of my heart' by Paul Baloche (various versions available from www.itunes.com)
- fruit flavoured sweets or jellies (be aware of allergies and intolerances)
- a bowl of fresh fruit (be aware of allergies and intolerances)
- fruit scented candles or air fresheners (be aware of safety issues, allergies etc)
- items from the Explore Together basic kit (see page 5)

Presenting the Bible

With the community gathered together, begin by sharing the words from Galatians 5:17–26. Consider carefully which version of the Bible you choose to read from.

Without being tempted to answer them, introduce the following questions to your community for them to consider:

- **What might God want to say to you today?**
- **What do you want to say to God?**
- **How are you allowing God to bear fruit in your life?**
- **Where do you need God's help your life?**

Pray

Pray for and with your community, asking God to help you hear from him. This time of prayer can be creative, interactive, responsive, meditative or sung. It could also include communion and intercession. Ensure that there is a place set aside where people can go if they feel that they need someone to pray with them specifically. Have a small team of people available to offer prayer if required. Prayer ministry should be available throughout an Explore Together session.

Explore

Read out your questions from Step 2 again or display them on a screen. Remind your community to consider these questions as they separate into their explore zones. Some may choose to consider all the questions while others may focus on just one. Some may completely ignore the questions and just open themselves up to God.

Invite your community to separate into small groups, around the zone(s) of their preference. Explain that individuals are welcome to spend as much or as little time in each zone as they wish, engaging at whatever level they feel comfortable. Depending upon where your quiet zone is located, you may wish to provide directions and remind people not to disturb one another when using this space.

Colour Zone
- coloured chalk sticks and black paper
- coloured pastels, crayons and white paper
- many different coloured pieces of fabric
- 'The fruit of the Spirit' image collection
- copies of the 'The fruit of the Spirit' ET questions

Word Zone

- pens, pencils, paper
- biblical commentaries relating to Galatians 5:17–26
- 'The fruit of the Spirit' word collection
- children's Bibles and Bible story books containing a version of Galatians 5:17–26
- copies of Galatians 5:17–26 (CEV) or Bibles
- copies of the 'The fruit of the Spirit' ET questions

Listening Zone
- MP3 players with the song 'Open the eyes of my heart' by Paul Baloche
- audio versions of different translations of Galatians 5:17–26
- copies of the 'The fruit of the Spirit' ET questions

Busy Zone
- pipe cleaners
- junk modelling items
- fruit flavoured sweets or jellies (be aware of allergies and intolerances)
- a bowl of fresh fruit (be aware of allergies and intolerances)
- copies of the 'The fruit of the Spirit' ET questions

Chat Zone
- a separate area with chairs, cushions or beanbags
- a chat zone host who is willing to read the passage again and then lead a discussion around the questions
- copies of Galatians 5:17–26 (CEV) or Bibles
- copies of the 'The fruit of the Spirit' ET questions

Quiet Zone
- 'The fruit of the Spirit' image collection (optional)
- fruit scented candles or air fresheners (be aware of safety issues, allergies etc)
- copies of Galatians 5:17–26 (CEV) or Bibles
- copies of the 'The fruit of the Spirit' ET questions

Share

As your time for exploring together draws to a close, invite your community to come back together into small groups of three to five. Suggest that they share their responses to the questions posed at the beginning.

Giving thanks

Invite the explorers to share their reflections with the wider community, drawing together their responses and noting any common themes that emerge. Conclude by sharing Galatians 5:17–26 as a benediction (using the same Bible version as before).Then lead your community in a prayer, thanking God for all that he has revealed through this story. Encourage your community to continue their conversations about this story as they leave, and to take with them any artwork/writings/thoughts from the session.

God looks on the inside

1 Samuel 16:1–13 Themes: priorities, judgement, appearance, integrity, faithfulness, trust

When God tells Samuel to go and look for a new king, Samuel automatically assumes the best looking and strongest man is the one he is searching for, but the Lord gently reminds Samuel that he is far more interested in what is happening on the inside…

Prepare

Resources required
- 'David the shepherd boy' audio recording (from *The Big Bible Storybook* audio book)
- 'God looks on the inside' image collection
- 'God looks on the inside' word collection
- 1 Samuel 16:1–13 (CEV)
- 'God looks on the inside' Explore Together questions (PDF and PowerPoint)

All available from www.exploretogether.org/downloads (using the code from the bottom of page 32).

You will also need to gather:
- audio versions of different translations of 1 Samuel 16:1–13
- copies of *David* board book (Scripture Union, 2012) (optional)
- sequins, feathers and strips of coloured paper
- small heart-shaped boxes to decorate
- eye masks (optional)
- items from the Explore Together basic kit (see page 5)
- someone to deliver a short sermon on 1 Samuel 16:1–13 (optional)

Presenting the Bible

With the community gathered together, begin by sharing the words from 1 Samuel 16:1–13. Consider carefully which version of the Bible you choose to read from.

Without being tempted to answer them, introduce the following questions to your community for them to consider:

- **What does this passage teach you about God?**
- **What might God be saying to you?**
- **What might God want you to change in your life?**
- **How does it feel to know that God looks into our hearts?**

Pray

Pray for and with your community, asking God to help you hear from him. This time of prayer can be creative, interactive, responsive, meditative or sung. It could also include communion and intercession. Ensure that there is a place set aside where people can go if they feel that they need someone to pray with them specifically. Have a small team of people available to offer prayer if required. Prayer ministry should be available throughout an Explore Together session.

Explore

Read out your questions from Step 2 again or display them on a screen. Remind your community to consider these questions as they separate into their explore zones. Some may choose to consider all the questions while others may focus on just one. Some may completely ignore the questions and just open themselves up to God.

Invite your community to separate into small groups, around the zone(s) of their preference. Explain that individuals are welcome to spend as much or as little time in each zone as they wish, engaging at whatever level they feel comfortable. Depending upon where your quiet zone is located, you may wish to provide directions and remind people not to disturb one another when using this space.

Colour Zone

- pens, pencils and crayons
- paper of various colours and sizes
- sticks of chalk and black paper
- 'God looks on the inside' image collection
- copies of the 'God looks on the inside' ET questions

Listening Zone
- 'David the shepherd boy' audio recording (from *The Big Bible Storybook* audio book)
- audio versions of different translations of 1 Samuel 16:1–13
- someone to deliver a short sermon on 1 Samuel 16:1–13 (optional)
- copies of the 'God looks on the inside' ET questions

Chat Zone
- a separate area with chairs, cushions or beanbags
- a chat zone host who is willing to read the passage again and then lead a discussion around the questions
- copies of 1 Samuel 16:1–13 (CEV) or Bibles
- copies of the 'God looks on the inside' ET questions

Word Zone

- pens, pencils, paper
- biblical commentaries relating to 1 Samuel 16:1–13
- 'God looks on the inside' word collection
- copies of *David* board book (Scripture Union, 2012), or other children's Bibles and Bible story books containing a version of 1 Samuel 16:1–13
- copies of 1 Samuel 16:1–13 (CEV) or Bibles
- copies of the 'God looks on the inside' ET questions

Busy Zone
- scissors, glue, masking tape
- pipe cleaners
- sequins, feathers and strips of coloured paper
- small heart-shaped boxes to decorate
- copies of the 'God looks on the inside' ET questions

Quiet Zone
- a separate area where people can be alone with their thoughts and God
- 'God looks on the inside' image collection (optional)
- eye masks (optional)
- copies of 1 Samuel 16:1–13 (CEV) or Bibles
- copies of the 'God looks on the inside' ET questions

Share

As your time for exploring together draws to a close, invite your community to come back together into small groups of three to five. Suggest that they share their responses to the questions posed at the beginning.

Giving thanks

Invite the explorers to share their reflections with the wider community, drawing together their responses and noting any common themes that emerge. Conclude by reading 1 Samuel 16:1–13 again (from the same Bible version used earlier). Then lead your community in a prayer, thanking God for all that he has revealed through this story. Encourage your community to continue their conversations about this story as they leave, and to take with them any artwork/writings/thoughts from the session.

Knowing God

Isaiah 11:1–9

Themes: knowing God, honouring God, holiness, prophecy, the Messiah, God's power

Sometimes God seems so far away it's almost impossible to imagine knowing him in the way we know one another. God sent Jesus to earth so that we might know him more deeply than ever before. In Isaiah's words we see a glimpse of the promised Messiah and what he will be like.

Prepare

Resources required
- 'I wonder' poem text
- 'I wonder' poem audio recording
- 'Knowing God' image collection
- 'Knowing God' word collection
- Isaiah 11:1–9 (CEV)
- 'Knowing God' Explore Together questions (PDF and PowerPoint)

All available from www.exploretogether.org/downloads (using the code from the bottom of page 32).

You will also need to gather:
- ribbons and flags of various colours and lengths
- gold and silver paper
- 'My Jesus, my Saviour' by Darlene Zschech (various versions available from www.itunes.com)
- ribbons and flags for dancing with
- animal and plant-shaped dough cutters
- items from the Explore Together basic kit (see page 5)
- a person willing to share their testimony, focusing on what they 'know' about God (optional)

Presenting the Bible

With the community gathered together, begin by sharing the words from Isaiah 11:1–9. Consider carefully which version of the Bible you choose to read from.

Alternatively or in addition you may choose to do the following:
- present this Bible passage using alternative media such as video, dance, art, dramatic reading etc

Without being tempted to answer them, introduce the following questions to your community for them to consider:

- **What does this passage teach us about God?**
- **What do you want to say to God?**
- **What have you learned that you didn't know before?**
- **How well do you know God already?**

Pray

Pray for and with your community, asking God to help you hear from him. This time of prayer can be creative, interactive, responsive, meditative or sung. It could also include communion and intercession. Ensure that there is a place set aside where people can go if they feel that they need someone to pray with them specifically. Have a small team of people available to offer prayer if required. Prayer ministry should be available throughout an Explore Together session.

Explore

Read out your questions from Step 2 again or display them on a screen. Remind your community to consider these questions as they separate into their explore zones. Some may choose to consider all the questions while others may focus on just one. Some may completely ignore the questions and just open themselves up to God.

Invite your community to separate into small groups, around the zone(s) of their preference. Explain that individuals are welcome to spend as much or as little time in each zone as they wish, engaging at whatever level they feel comfortable. Depending upon where your quiet zone is located, you may wish to provide directions and remind people not to disturb one another when using this space.

Colour Zone
- pens, pencils, crayons and pastels
- paper of varying sizes and colours
- scissors and glue
- gold and silver paper
- 'Knowing God' image collection
- copies of the 'Knowing God' ET questions

Listening Zone
- MP3 players with a version of 'My Jesus, my Saviour' by Darlene Zschech
- 'I wonder' poem audio recording
- audio versions of different translations of Isaiah 11:1–9
- a person willing to share their testimony, focusing on what they 'know' about God (optional)
- copies of the 'Knowing God' ET questions

Chat Zone

- a separate area with chairs, cushions or beanbags
- a chat zone host who is willing to read the passage again and then lead a discussion around the questions
- copies of Isaiah 11:1–9 (CEV) or Bibles
- copies of the 'Knowing God' ET questions

Word Zone
- pens, pencils, paper
- sticky notes
- biblical commentaries relating to Isaiah 11:1–9
- 'Knowing God' word collection
- copies of 'I wonder' poem text
- children's Bibles and Bible story books containing a version of Isaiah 11:1–9
- copies of Isaiah 11:1–9 (CEV) or Bibles
- copies of the 'Knowing God' ET questions

Busy Zone

- plasticine, play dough or clay
- junk modelling items
- ribbons and flags for dancing with
- animal and plant-shaped dough cutters
- copies of the 'Knowing God' ET questions

Quiet Zone
- a separate area where people can be alone with their thoughts and God
- 'Knowing God' image collection (optional)
- copies of Isaiah 11:1–9 (CEV) or Bibles
- copies of the 'Knowing God' ET questions

Share

As your time for exploring together draws to a close, invite your community to come back together into small groups of three to five. Suggest that they share their responses to the questions posed at the beginning.

Giving thanks

Invite the explorers to share their reflections with the wider community, drawing together their responses and noting any common themes that emerge. Conclude by reading Isaiah 11:1–9 again (from the same Bible version used earlier). Then lead your community in a prayer, thanking God for all that he has revealed through this story. Encourage your community to continue their conversations about this story as they leave, and to take with them any artwork/writings/thoughts from the session.

Frequently asked questions

Does Explore Together negate the need for age-specific ministry?

The practice of Explore Together embodies the principle that a multigenerational community can engage with God's Word, learn from each other and grow together.

It is also true that within age-specific ministries there can be diversity of thought, rich experience and God-given creativity for sharing. Explore Together is a rare tool that can be used to nourish all-age community as well as enhance those ministries aimed at specific age-groups.

Although some churches do take and use Explore Together as a discrete part of their monthly programme, many churches use it to enrich their existing activities. The beauty of Explore Together is that it can be used within children's groups, youth groups, house groups, school groups, Bible study groups, outreach groups or even within the family home – in fact, anywhere that the Bible is shared. Its benefits are not restricted to all-age services.

We are a very traditional church community. How could Explore Together work within our traditions?

Explore Together embraces tradition but also pushes the boundaries that can be imposed by those traditions. It can fit neatly into the traditional order of things and can also be the catalyst that takes the community on an additional adventure.

Explore Together can be used to help people understand and interpret the meaning and value of symbol and tradition. A whole range of churches from a number of different traditions have taken and used it in different ways. It offers flexibility for churches and communities to make the time of exploring their own, using it so that it fits their group of people.

Our church has many people/a few people. Will it work here?

Over the last five years we have seen Explore Together used in small groups with only a few individuals and also in larger settings. We have known Explore Together to be used within a family home, and also within a programme at Spring Harvest for 450 children.

Key to the smooth running of Explore Together is preparation and planning. It is important to consider how the participants will arrange themselves into small groups. There is a danger that individuals who are close friends, or of similar age and background, will organise themselves into groups, therefore missing out on the excellent opportunity to learn from those who are a different age or stage in their lives. Inclusivity is key if individuals want to be challenged to learn something new.

While the planning, organisation and setting up of the zones are essential, large or small numbers of people do not present a challenge. No matter how large the group is, Step 5: Share is always done in small groups of three to five people. When feeding back in larger churches or groups, having a group of people with roving radio microphones in the congregation works very well.

Isn't Explore Together a bit chaotic, especially with children present?

It is chaotic in the sense that everyone is engaging in different ways, but not because the children are present. The explore zones are designed to embrace a range of learning preferences. Individuals of all ages very quickly find their own preferred activity and become occupied. Although there might be a buzz in the room, activity will be purposeful, colourful and appealing, and everyone has the freedom to move around and make choices in a safe and supportive environment. Many adults find the kinaesthetic dimension of Explore Together appealing too!

Does Explore Together need a lot of space? We have fixed pews in our church building that often restrict what we can do

Explore Together can be planned carefully to fit flexibly into spaces that are different in size and organised in different ways. The explore zones do not all need to happen in one room, they could be spread out to happen in different areas. Your choice of activities can also be tailored to the amount of space you have, and you can creatively use the edges and corners of a room that contains pews. The smallest setting for Explore Together that we have heard about is at a dining room table in a family home.

I find sharing my ideas and thoughts very daunting. Do I really have to share my answers? Will others pressure me into talking?

The value of small groups is significant. Individuals have the opportunity to share what they have discovered, and shape the views, thinking and experiences of each other.

It is important that small groups are 'safe places', and that key expectations for how those groups will function are shared. Small groups need to be a place where individuals might not speak. There is huge value in being part of a small group and simply listening. Small groups also need to be a place where people can freely make mistakes, a place where original thoughts and ideas are encouraged. Some individuals might benefit from talking their ideas through one-to-one with another before sharing in a group, but others may never do so.

Individuals within groups need to be careful not to add to pressure others might feel. It should never be an expectation that everyone will talk.

Is Explore Together an alternative to Messy Church?

Messy Church and Explore Together complement each other in many ways. Explore Together can be used as a way of engaging with the Bible within any context. It is just one way of exploring the Bible 'in community'.

Messy Church is a Fresh Expression of church developed to encourage new congregations previously out of reach of 'traditional' church. Rather than replace Messy Church, Explore Together could be used within a Messy Church congregation. In his book *Making Disciples in Messy Church*, Paul Moore mentions that there is a lack of discipleship resources specifically designed for adults and children to

use together in an all-age context, like Messy Church, or in the family home. We would strongly suggest that Explore Together ticks that box.

How inclusive is Explore Together for individuals with disabilities and learning difficulties?

Individuals with disabilities and learning difficulties have been involved in Explore Together since its inception. Those with physical difficulties, Down syndrome, diagnoses of ADHD and autistic spectrum conditions have all participated. Individuals are able to express their personal skills, interests and abilities in the explore zones. They can focus on tasks for a length of time that fits their capabilities, and they can share their answers in verbal and nonverbal ways.

It is important to eliminate barriers to participation when planning. For example, if your church or group has members with physical disabilities it is a good idea to ensure that materials and activities are placed at a suitable height. For others, you might wish to use a visual timetable to help an individual know what will be happening next and to show the choices that are available to them in the explore zones.

Explore Together is a scary concept for our church. Is there any way we can implement it in stages?

The key to using Explore Together is to get to know and trust it. Using Explore Together in a smaller group setting to start with helps to build confidence and gets people involved. Using it in a house group setting or with a Sunday school group provides the ideal environment for becoming familiar with the process – children are so much more receptive to new ideas than adults!

We started using Explore Together with a small group of 5 to 11s. Other members of the children's team were involved and experienced first hand its effectiveness. From there we gained the confidence to share what we did in Sunday school with the wider church community. What started within a small group of children has now been used with 450 8 to

11-years-olds at Spring Harvest and in large national intergenerational events, too. If you need to, start small, but don't be afraid to grow.

How can Explore Together help adults who are reluctant to get out of the pew to engage?

The first thing to establish in situations like this is: Why the reluctance? If the reason concerns mobility and access then measures can be taken to make sure that all areas are easily available or, in extreme cases, the resources can be brought to the person.

More often than not the reluctance comes from the fear of change. The very nature of Explore Together is to provide an environment where every person can engage with the Bible in a way that embraces their natural preferences. There is quite literally something for everyone – the key is making sure that Explore Together is understood before it is forced upon a community that could be less than receptive.

If there are only one or two people for whom change may be difficult, take some time to sit down and explain what you plan to do and why you are doing it. There should be no pressure for people to go to a zone. One of the options is to reflect on the Bible passage quietly, and people could do this by staying in their seats; another is to deliver a sermon in the listening zone.

If the community is filled with people who are reluctant to leave their pews then maybe Explore Together in zone format is not right for you at this time. An alternative option would be to provide a bag (brown paper takeaway bags are ideal) for each person. The bag would contain a small notebook, a pen, a pack of coloured pencils, a small tub of play dough, some images relating to the Bible passage, a copy of the Bible passage or a Bible and a copy of the questions. The process would be the same, except that the community remains seated while they explore. The sharing time would be with those seated around them, and the feedback would happen in the same way as in the original format. This is less than ideal but it could be a stepping stone.

There will need to be a point at which a decision to move forward needs to be taken. Explore Together is a tool created to encourage people to discover the truths of the Bible for themselves. It is another pathway to a deeper relationship with God, intended to help people grow in their faith and reach maturity. Reluctance to engage should be seen as a pastoral opportunity to come alongside that person; to identify barriers and begin to break them down with prayer and persistence. Discipleship is never a done deal, it is a continuous journey that needs to take place in community. It also requires us to address and not ignore telltale signs that indicate the need for intervention – part of being a biblical community is to take that responsibility seriously (Colossians 1:28; 3:16). Explore Together helps to identify where on that journey we are and where help is needed.

What if someone says something completely off-the-wall?

Our immediate response to this question is, 'It's better out than in.' What better place is there to explore your faith and ask your questions than in a community of faith – a community made up of many people with varying levels of understanding, wisdom, knowledge and experience? Explore Together provides a safe environment for people to express their thoughts and ideas, some of which may otherwise never be aired or challenged. The questions help to provide safe boundaries and keep the focus on the desirable aims and outcomes.

The web resources for the sessions in this book are available from:
www.exploretogether.org/downloads

Your access code is: 3xPLor3t0g3THr2